Stock Trading Riches:
The Simple, but Powerful
Formula that Transforms
Your Stock Picks into Money Pumps

By

Praveen Puri

The author and publisher shall have neither liability nor responsibility to any person or entity with respect to any loss or damage caused, or alleged to be caused, directly or indirectly by the information contained in this book. The information, methods and techniques described by the author are based on his own experience.

They may not work for you and no recommendation is made to follow the same course of action. No representation is made that following the advice in this book will work in your case. The author and publisher expressly disclaim any and all warranties, including but not limited to warranty of fitness for particular use.

Everyone's financial situation is different. This book is designed to provide information in regard to the subject matter covered. It is sold with the understanding that the publisher and author are not engaged in rendering legal, accounting, financial planning, or other professional services.

With regard to the stock examples in this book, remember that past performance is no guarantee of success.

Author's Note: 2009 Updates

Like a trader developing a trading system, a writer has to discipline himself to reach a feeling of satisfaction with his work, and then just learn to accept it as is – without any further tinkering.

The Zen concept of "perfectly imperfect".

So I never planned to update "Stock Trading Riches".

However, during the two years since this book was first published, I have received a lot of feedback from readers.

Mostly, they were excited and enthusiastic about my system, but I noticed four areas of concern:

1. How did my system stand up during the severe recession? Is this the time to trade or invest?

2. Could I provide an Excel spreadsheet for my formula?

3. Can my system be used with mutual funds, even though I mentioned that I don't use them?

4. Would I provide more advice on stock and market analysis?

As a result, I have created a new section, which has been appended to the original book (after page 58).

This book is dedicated to:

My wife, Rasika

And

My son, Anshul

Table of Contents

Preface

This book contains my simple and elegant stock market trading system.

It does not require a lot of time, effort, and special knowledge, and it can give you a great return without undue risk.

I love trading with my system, and am proud of it.

Trading my system allows me to express my passion for simplicity, elegance, minimalism, Zen, and present-moment awareness. Practicing it feels like a form of meditation.

This is not a "black box" system. I do not want you to just take my rules and follow them blindly. I want you to understand my system, test it, modify it, and make it your own.

Your trading will be much more fun and productive when you have a system that you love and trust.

Part I – Laying the Foundation

Introduction

I have had a lot of financial and trading experience:

- I have been trading my own account for almost 20 years.

- As a consultant for a large insurance company, I helped design and implement custom software for tracking a $30 billion investment portfolio.

- As a consultant at the Chicago Board of Trade (CBOT), I helped support and develop their "Project A" electronic trading platform.

- I am currently a vice president at a major bank, where I support and develop FX systems for corporate clients.

In the last couple of years, I have become passionate about sharing my stock trading system with others.

When I was starting out, I was like any other new trader.

I made less than I should have because I kept switching from one system to another.

I spent thousands of dollars on courses, books, videos, and seminars.

I learned all about trend following, technical analysis, patterns, and charting techniques.

But, in the end, I was not happy with my results…

Brutal Fact

I realized that:

99% of all systems use the same old indicators.
99% of all trading books say "the trend is your friend".
99% of traders fail to beat the markets.

The brutal fact is that a free market is about price discovery. A market works like an organism - "consuming" new fundamental and technical information and rendering it ineffective.

A 30-day moving average may make money for a while. Then the market will "digest" this parameter, and a 65-day moving average may become the new money-maker.

Today's report on CNBC is already reflected in the price of the stock.

Only 1% of traders are superstars who can consistently find, re-adjust and exploit new information.

Less is More

I gave away all my trading books, and started a self-evaluation process.

My natural obsession with simplicity and minimalism kicked in, and I started gravitating towards simpler systems.

I realized that The Big Secret for the "little guy" trader is simplicity.

You need a system that is flexible and robust – that does not depend on the market moving in trends, or creating chart patterns.

True Story:

In the summer of 2007, Forbes Magazine sponsored an off-road race over hilly terrain between a Ford Model-T and a Hummer. Guess which won?

The Model-T kicked the Hummer's butt!

The Model-T was designed with rugged, ingenious simplicity.

Zen Simplicity

I then became fascinated with the idea of a pure Zen trading system. It would use no news reports, indicators, charts, or parameters to distract you from Now. It would be able to handle any market condition.

I turned to jazz, improvisation, Taoism, simplicity, and minimalism for inspiration.

I ended up building a simple and minimalist trading system around an old, obscure, 19th century Wall Street formula called *constant value investing*.

A Successful Trader

Since I developed my system, I can hardly describe how my trading career has changed.

While I'm no financial genius like Warren Buffet, I have made a double-digit annual return for years now.

I use no indicators or charts.

Those are nothing but crutches that keep you hobbling around, instead of surfing in the flow with the market.

I simply do an easy "back of the envelope" calculation for each of my stocks.

Analog in a Digital World

To understand my system, it helps to shift your mind-set from digital thinking to analog.

A digital system has two values (i.e. yes or no), while an analog system has a range of values. For example, a computer memory bit can only be off or on, but your oven can be set to a range of temperatures.

Normally, we trade digitally. After we buy a stock, we either hold it or sell it. So, for the trade to make us money, we only have one chance to buy the stock correctly, and then one chance to sell it correctly.

My trading system is analog.   After you initially buy into a stock, the constant value formula automatically uses feedback to adjust the position – buying and selling portions of your holdings. It works like a self-correcting gyro control in a torpedo.

Part II – My Simple Trading System

Appearances are Deceiving

Before we look at the constant value formula, I should give a warning: It might *appear* that the formula is too simple, and you might feel a let-down ("Is that all there is?").

But I *assure* you that, beneath the bare minimal surface, there is power.

Like chess, the rules are easy to understand, but mastery is illusive.

Now, let's look at the constant value formula...

The "Magic" Formula

Here are the rules for constant value investing:

1. *Buy a certain dollar's worth of a stock or fund.*

2. *Rebalance back to this constant value on a periodic basis (i.e. yearly, quarterly, or monthly).*

3. *Do not rebalance unless the value has changed at least ± 10%.*

4. *After sales, the proceeds go into the cash pool.*

5. *Purchases are made from the cash pool. If the cash pool is depleted, we add cash.*

For example, let's assume that you buy $10,000 of mutual fund ABC. One year later, the fund is up 12% and your stake is worth $11,200. You would then sell $1,200 worth of the fund and would now have $10,000 in the fund and $1,200 in cash.

Now let's assume that, after another year, the fund is down 10%, and you now have $9,000 worth of ABC. You would then invest $1,000 from your pool of cash. Now, you have $10,000 in ABC and $200 cash, for a total of $10,200.

If you would have just held your initial $10,000 in ABC, it would now be worth $10,080 (all stock, no cash). In this case, the difference is only $120 but, over longer periods, and wider swings, the cash really starts to build.

If you are applying constant value investing to a stock or exchange traded fund, you cannot buy or sell in exact dollar amounts.

Instead, you divide the constant amount by the latest share price and then round down to find the number of shares you need to own. Then you buy or sell enough shares to reach this number.

For example, let us say that you want to maintain $10,000 in stock XYZ. At first, it is trading at $20/share, so you buy 10000/20 = 500 shares. If it then trades at $35.46/share, you now want to own 10000/35.46 = 282 shares (rounded down). So, you would now sell 218 shares (500 - 282).

Keep in mind that, while the constant value formula is the heart of my trading system, it is insufficient by itself. Anything can happen to an individual stock.

As we shall see in a later chapter, my system applies constant value to a portfolio of stocks. The formula takes advantage of each stock's volatility, while the portfolio handles risk, diversification, and growth.

The Formula's Hidden Power

As I mentioned before, constant value is a very simple formula. So simple that it is easy to dismiss it. But, this formula is profound and very powerful.

It embodies the Eastern principles of *Now* and *No preferences*.

We do not have to worry about "timing" the stock. If we initially buy in at a higher price, the formula self-corrects the stock position over time. This means that we can concentrate on picking good companies.

It makes no difference what a stock's past or future prices are. If we are rebalancing a stock to $10,000, and it is now at $5 / share, we want to own 2,000 shares. It doesn't matter if the price was previously at $2 or $30. It does not matter if the next price will be $8 or $100.

We have no expectations. We are in a very powerful position. The market can't "digest" our system – because our system even works with random noise.

For us, the stock market no longer trends in time. It has become a series of independent Present Moments – strung together like pearls.

Actual Trading Example

Here are Amazon.com (AMZN) split-adjusted prices for the first trading day in each January, from 2000 to 2007:

2000 $64.56

2001 $17.31

2002 $14.19

2003 $21.85

2004 $50.40

2005 $43.22

2006 $44.82

2007 $37.31

The prices are from BarChart.com.

Let's pretend that we initially invested $2,000 in Amazon.com (AMZN) in January, 2000.

This was the _WORST possible time_ – just before the dot-com bubble burst. We would have bought 30 shares at $64.56.

Then, we rebalanced back to $2000 at the start of each January by dividing 2000 by the current share price (and rounding down) to find out how many shares we needed to own. We added new cash for purchases when necessary.

Here are the buys/sells that the formula would have recommended on the first trading day of each year:

2001	Buy 85 shares	@ $17.31
2002	Buy 25 shares	@ $14.19
2003	Sell 49 shares	@ $21.85
2004	Sell 52 shares	@ $50.40
2005	Buy 7 shares	@ $43.22
2006	* No Trade	
2007	Buy 7 shares	@ $37.31

Here is a table showing a snapshot, at each price, of the number of shares owned, cash on hand, total value (stock plus cash), and total investment:

price	shares	cash pool	total value	amount invested
$64.56	30	$63.20	$2,000.00	$2,000.00
$17.31	115	$0.00	$1,990.65	$3,408.15
$14.19	140	$0.00	$1,986.6	$3,762.90
$21.85	91	$1,070.65	$3,059.00	$3,762.90
$50.40	39	$3,691.45	$5,657.05	$3,762.90
$43.22	46	$3,388.91	$5,377.03	$3,762.90
*$44.82	46	$3,388.91	$5,450.63	$3,762.90
$37.31	53	$3,127.74	$5,105.17	$3,762.90

Even though AMZN _went down 42%_ from 2000 to 2007, we are _up 36%._

The constant value formula mechanically "self-corrected" our bad timing.

There are 2 other things to notice:

First, even though AMZN went through a "doomsday scenario", and plunged 73% in 2001, we only had to invest another $1,408.15.

Because we diversify among stocks, and avoid leverage, we can handle anything the market does. Think jazz riffs, Taoism, and improvisation.

Secondly, notice that the constant value formula got us near the break-even point in 2003 – even though AMZN was still 66% below our initial purchase price!

Complete System Rules

❖ I want to own a constant value of as many positions as possible. I only use one cash pool for the portfolio.

❖ I only invest in stocks, exchange traded funds (ETFs), or closed-end funds. I do not invest in regular mutual funds, options, or futures.

❖ I may sell an individual stock if it is heading towards bankruptcy but, for the most part, I want to hold my stocks forever, or until they are taken away from me (i.e. mergers, etc).

❖ I use Scottrade because they only charge $7 / trade.

❖ For now, I have chosen $2000 as my constant value for each stock. I may change this value in the future, as my account grows.

❖ I chose $2000 because it is big enough for fluctuations, but small enough that I can contribute this amount most months. Also, if an individual company went bankrupt, I wouldn't be hurt too badly.

❖ I try to contribute $2000/month to my account. So, I try to buy a new stock each month.

❖ When I first started my account, I put in an additional $2000 to start the cash pool.

❖ If I add a large lump sum, I would add 30% to the cash pool (i.e. only buy positions with 70%).

❖ I rebalance my positions only once a year, at the end of December – as long as they have changed at least ± 10%.

❖ My testing has indicated that more frequent rebalancing is not worth it. *__The hardest part of my system is to resist tinkering and rebalancing after big drops or rises.__*

❖ When rebalancing, I handle the sales first, to build up the cash pool for buys.

❖ In November, I estimate if the cash pool will run short. In that case, I don't buy stocks with my November and December contributions.

❖ If I still need cash, I'll add more. If there was a really bad stock market crash, and I was still short, I would sell off a few of the worst stocks to raise more cash.

❖ Since the stock market mostly goes up, the long term problem is too much cash. So, I cap the maximum % of cash in my account to 30%, and use the excess cash to buy more stocks. *__My portfolio experiences compound growth, while the stocks work like money pumps, going up and down.__*

❖ I get my stock picks from Forbes, Yahoo.com, MSN.com, newspapers, etc. I want to buy growth or value stocks that will be around. The constant value formula will self-correct the timing, in case I buy the stock too high.

Commissions

Some people think that using my system will result in excess commissions.

This is not true.

As I mentioned in the previous chapter, I use Scottrade as my broker. By trading through their website, I only get charged $7 per trade.

Remember that I keep $2,000 in each position and only rebalance once a year.

If my account was 100% invested, and all my positions fluctuated at least 10%, my yearly expense would be 7 / 2000 = 0.35%. That is less than managed funds, and is competitive with index funds.

In practice, my expense is less than 0.35% because some of the account is in cash, and not all positions fluctuate 10%.

Because of the growth of my account, I will eventually increase my constant value. Then, my expense ratio will be even lower.

I would not recommend that you keep less than $2,000 per position.

If this means that you will not be able to hold many positions, then, for safety, you should either invest mainly in ETFs or use the stop loss variation discussed later in this book.

Taxes

Now, let's discuss taxes.

Obviously, they will not be a problem in tax-free or tax-deferred accounts.

However, my biggest account is taxable, and I have no problems there either, because my system has tax advantages.

First, we need to discuss cost basis.

The cost basis is what you subtract from the sale price to determine if you have a profit or loss.

For example, let's assume that you sell 10 shares of a stock at $15 / share, and get $150. If you had paid $7 each for those 10 shares, your cost basis is $70, and your profit is $80.

If you bought all your shares in a particular stock or fund at the same price, your cost basis is simple.

However, if you buy shares at different prices, then the IRS gives you a choice of different ways of calculating your basis.

For example, with regular mutual funds, you can average your cost basis. If you bought ½ your shares at $20, and ½ your shares at $10, you can claim a cost basis for all your shares as $15.

You are not, however, allowed to average the cost for stocks or ETFs. You have to track each purchase separately.

So, if you sell some stock, how do you know which batch you sold? Two of the methods that the IRS allows you to use are "first in, first out" (FIFO) or "last in, first out" (LIFO). You can pick either method.

With LIFO, you sell your shares in the _reverse order_ that you bought them.

For example, let's say that, one year ago, you bought 10 shares at $12. Then, last month, you bought 5 more shares at $14.

If you now sell 10 shares, your cost basis for the first 5 shares will be $14, and the next 5 will have a cost basis of $12. After the sale, you are now left with 5 shares at $12.

With FIFO, you sell your shares in the _order_ that you bought them.

For example, let's again say that, one year ago, you bought 10 shares at $12. Then, last month, you bought 5 more shares at $14.

If you now sell 10 shares, your cost basis for all 10 shares will be $12. After the sale, you are now left with 5 shares at $14.

The first tax advantage occurs because the constant value formula is _guaranteed to produce a LIFO profit, but can have a FIFO loss._

For example, let's pretend that we buy into stock ABC at $20.

If we now rebalance at $8, we will buy more shares. If ABC then goes to $14, we sell shares. Since $14 is greater than $8, we have made a LIFO profit.

However, since $14 is less than $20, we have a FIFO loss.

I always use FIFO for tax purposes.

Since my "money pumps" (i.e. stocks) are fluctuating independently of each other, I will usually have some FIFO losses to offset FIFO gains at tax time, even though all the positions will eventually produce LIFO gains!

Because I rebalance only once a year (and use the FIFO method), most of my profits are long term capital gains. These are thus taxed at a lower rate than regular income. This is a second tax advantage.

There is a third tax advantage that I don't use, because I want to hold onto my positions. But you might want to take advantage of it.

You get this advantage when you rebalance a down position by selling it completely and buying a new stock. Then, you get a larger loss to offset your gains.

For example, let's pretend that you bought $2,000 worth of GM, and it is now worth $1600.

Instead of rebalancing GM back to $2,000 (by buying another $400's worth), you could sell all your GM, have a $400 capital loss for your taxes, and buy $2,000 worth of Ford.

The trick here is that you don't want to violate the IRS "wash rule". If you sell a stock at a loss and deduct it, you can't buy the same stock back for 30 days. So, you would have to either buy a completely new stock, or one from the same sector.

Part III – Optional Ideas for Customizing the System

<u>Variation 1 – Constant Value</u>

The first way to customize my system is by changing the constant value.

In my case, I keep things simple by having one constant value for every position.

Currently, I have set it at $2,000 so that I can diversify.

When I get to a point where I feel that I have too many positions, I will probably increase it.

But, there is no reason that you have to use $2,000 – or even one constant value.

You could, for example, keep $100,000 in an S&P 500 ETF, and use $40,000 to invest in 10 small companies.

You would then rebalance the ETF to $100,000, and each company to $4,000.

Variation 2 – Cash Levels

You can also customize my trading system by varying the cash pool.

In my case, since I am saving and investing on a monthly basis, I use my full contribution towards buying a position.

I know that, if my cash pool is inadequate, I can use future monthly contributions for rebalancing.

If, on the other hand, I was contributing a large, one-time lump sum, I would put 30% of it in the cash pool.

So, for example, if I suddenly got $20,000 to invest, I would buy 7 new positions (for a total of $14,000) and save $6,000.

I also limit the cash pool to be, at most, 30% of the account value. I then use the extra cash to add more positions.

To customize, you can vary this percentage.

I would not exceed 50% cash. That would be the most conservative option.

Variation 3 – Rebalance Frequency

We can also customize the system by how frequently we rebalance.

During testing, I found that stocks enter volatile periods where monthly rebalancing would pay off but, at other times, they drift.

Stocks also undergo multi-year trends – such as the 1982-2000 bull market and 2000-2003 bear market. In those markets, we would optimally rebalance after several years.

Remember that we want a system that avoids optimized parameters. Markets change. We don't want to fall in the trap of switching between rebalancing frequencies.

I also diversify over a lot of positions. It would be too much work to monitor and rebalance all of them on a monthly basis.

Therefore, I feel that yearly rebalancing is the best solution.

But, I want you to develop a system that suits your own needs and temperament.

You may decide that weekly, monthly, or quarterly work better for you – especially since we require a minimum 10% move.

<u>Variation 4 – Percentage Trigger</u>

Instead of rebalancing yearly or monthly, you may want to use a percentage trigger.

For example, you may want to rebalance any position that moves up or down 15%.

You could even combine both methods:

Rebalance both yearly (if the position has moved at least 10% from the last rebalance point), and whenever the position moves more than 15%.

I personally keep things simple and do not use any of these variations. I'm happy with the basic system.

But, that does not mean there is no value to these ideas.

I would not be surprised if you designed your own system that outperformed my basic system.

Variation 5 – Constant Value Growth

In the basic system, we do not increase the constant value for each individual stock. Instead, we cap the maximum percentage of cash in the portfolio.

This way, our portfolio grows over time, while our individual positions stay the same.

As an alternative, you may want to increase your commitment to winning positions.

You can do this by increasing constant value whenever a stock has gone up from the last rebalancing. You compute a new constant value by averaging the current constant value with the current stock value.

For example, you buy 1,000 shares of ABC at $2 / share. You now have a constant value of 2,000.

If ABC goes down to $1 / share, the constant value stays at 2,000 and you now want to own 2,000 shares.

If ABC goes back up to $2 / share, your 2,000 shares are now worth $4,000. Under the basic rules, you would now sell $2,000 worth of stock.

Under the growth rules, the constant value will now become (4,000 + 2000) / 2 = 3,000. You would now sell $1,000 worth of stock.

If ABC then went down to $1 / share again, you would then want to own 3,000 shares.

There are three disadvantages with this rule:

First, you need to track separate constant values for all of your positions.

Second, some of your positions will become huge and overwhelm your portfolio. If and when these stocks crash or stagnate, they will tie up a lot of your funds.

Third, you are now trend-following.

I have pondered and tested this rule out, and I personally do not use it.

I want to keep my system simple and minimal.

I never want to favor any individual stock.

I only trust the present moment. I do not want to follow trends.

Variation 6 – Stop Loss Rule

I believe that my basic trading system has enough protection because I diversify, never increase the constant value, and take profits.

What if I had owned Enron?

First, it would have only represented $2,000.

Second, as the stock climbed in the go-go '90's, I would have been taking profits to build up my cash pool.

Third, Forbes Magazine and others warned of Enron before it went bankrupt. I would have had enough time to sell it (and buy a new $2,000 position) before it went out of business.

However, if you feel more comfortable trading with a stop-loss, you can add an optional rule:

Completely sell any position that falls 50% below your initial buy point, and replace it with a new position.

In our Amazon example, this rule would have caused us to sell out of our position.

Part IV – Zen and the Art of Speculation

How May I Serve The Market?

Trading is usually looked upon as a zero-sum battle, where you are competing against other traders.

I want you to replace that outlook to the market.

**Instead of seeing other market participants as competitors, you must begin to see them as your customers.**

This is the reason that my system has an edge.

You are serving other market participants (including traders) by buying low and selling high, thus properly fulfilling the role of a speculator.

Most people think of a speculator as a risky trader who bets big. But there is a different definition of a speculator in economics:

**The economic role of the speculator is to provide liquidity to a market, in order to balance supply / demand.**

When people want to sell, and the stock price declines, the constant value formula causes you to step in and mop up excess supply, which is then added to your inventory.

When people want to buy, and the stock price rises, the constant value formula causes you to step in and satisfy excess demand, by selling to them from your inventory.

Old School Discipline

Discipline is the one cliché in trading books that is true.

Once you have a trading system that gives you an edge in the markets, you need to *use* your system.

Not once. Not sometimes. All the time – no matter what the market is doing.

This is where having a simple system that you love and trust becomes essential. In real trading – with real money on the line – fear and greed is amplified.

If you aren't trading with a well-thought-out plan, or don't have 100% confidence, you will become stressed and make impulsive decisions.

This book devotes relatively few pages to the actual trading system – which is simple and minimal.

Instead, this book devotes a lot of pages to mental and philosophical ideas.

In the next couple of chapters, I will give sports and casino analogies.

Like a professional athlete, a trader needs to combine skill with the right mindset and attitude.

Like a casino, you need to ply your edge continually and unemotionally. You need to focus on the process, not on short terms wins and losses.

Defense! Defense!

Whenever I think about my system, I hear the roar of an NBA (basketball) crowd chanting "Defense! Defense!" when the visitors have the ball.

If my system was a basketball team, it would not be flashy, with lots of dunks and three-point shots.

Instead, my team would be focused on playing solid defense, passing the ball a lot, and having the open man take a high percentage shot.

If my system was a soccer team, I would see it playing a great backfield, hardly letting the opponent take a shot on goal.

My team would keep the ball on the opponent's side of the field, keeping them back, and causing scoring opportunities to appear.

If my system was used for golf, it would not call for taking big shots. Instead, you would be patient, playing for par, and taking birdie opportunities as they arose.

You would mentally "reset" yourself after a mistake, and trust that the system would self-correct it over time, by working with the course and your mistakes.

Smash Mouth Football

My trading system is like *simple, old school, smash-mouth Bears football.*

Run the ball, block hard, don't get fancy, and let your defense win the game. It works with the 99% who are hard-working, "lunch-pail" blue collar players.

Leave the fancy passing "West Coast" offensive systems for the 1% superstars like Joe Montana.

You win through defense. By selling when others are buying, and buying when others are selling, you get good "field position" – i.e. your inventory's cost basis falls over time.

Like Bears football, the greatest danger with my system is that you will either dismiss it as too simple and childish, or else you will become bored and lose interest in it. *My system requires discipline and patience, just like old school football.*

Knuckleball Dance

My trading system makes a lot of people uncomfortable.

Some feel exposed without charts, indicators, and expert opinions. Some are really uncomfortable about buying low and selling high, instead of trend-following.

I compare it to the "Zen of the Knuckleball" in baseball.

Most pitchers learn to throw fastballs, curves, sliders, and change-ups. Their main pitch is the fastball – brute force, throw it as hard as possible.

In every generation, there are a tiny minority who are "knuckleballers". They throw the knuckleball almost exclusively.

Unlike the other pitches that are thrown hard, a knuckleball is thrown softly. It "dances" in the air.

Instead of controlling the speed and location, the knuckleball pitcher has no control, and has no idea how the pitch will move.

Instead, he trusts the process.

He has faith that, even though the knuckleball is moving slowly, its path changes moment to moment, making it nearly impossible for the batter to track and time it.

With my system, I'm asking you to discard the other pitches, and start throwing the knuckleball...

Get Your Uniform Dirty

If my trading system was a baseball team, it would not be the flashy one that hit a lot of home runs.

Instead, my team would be the one with the dirty uniforms - with great pitching, defense, and fundamentals.

My team would play each "at bat" independently – without regard to whether it was a regular season or playoff game.

It might seem like my system is cutting your profits short. But, instead, you are choking up on the bat - reducing home runs, but also strikeouts.

We would win through drawing walks, scratching out infield singles, stealing bases, and executing hit and run plays...

Place Your Bets!

You can learn about the business of trading by observing a casino.

Unlike the patrons who are there for entertainment, the casino does not bet wildly, and ride a roller coaster of high and low emotions.

Instead, a casino develops an edge and uses it, unemotionally, over and over again.

They never try to make a killing overnight. That is why they have table limits.

If a patron wins big, they do not want revenge, and try to "get it back". They know they have an edge, and the win is good publicity.

They just want to stay in the game, and pound away with their edge.

My system has an economic edge, because it buys low and sells high to add liquidity to the marketplace.

I want to keep pounding away with this edge. So, I never risk too much on any one stock.

If a stock crashes, I gladly buy it cheaply and add it to my inventory.

I trust that the formula, combined with diversification and waiting once a year, will keep me from sinking too much money too early in a decline.

Conclusion

If someone had handed me this formula when I was younger, I would not have used it, because I wanted to get rich quick – I wanted "action" and triple-digit returns.

Now I understand that those kinds of systems are unsustainable.

Instead of becoming an instant millionaire on one spectacular day-trade, I now want to pass this formula down to my son as a legacy. He would use it to add on to the family wealth, and then pass it along to the next generation.

I hope that you, the reader, now have an appreciation for my system – and the ideas of simplicity and getting rich slowly but surely.

I wish you well on your journey, both as a trader and through life in general.

I want to leave you with a story…

The Mouse, Bird, and Fox

A haughty bird spotted a mouse crawling through the field.

The bird landed next to the mouse and said: "Oh, poor mouse! A hungry fox prowls this field! What are you going to do if he sees you?"

The mouse answered: "I have but one option – I will run away".

The bird boasted: "I know several ways to escape the fox!"

Just then, the fox arrived!

The mouse ran away, and the fox ate the bird while it tried to figure out which escape method to use.

Moral: It pays to keep things simple!

Part V – Bonus Scripts

Using the Scripts

As a bonus, this book includes both Awk and Perl scripts that implement my trading formula. These scripts are also posted on my Unix blog, http://unix-simple.blogspot.com/

These scripts will come in handy for testing the past performance of stocks or funds.

Free versions of Perl and Awk are available online, and free price data can be obtained from BarChart.com.

To use either of the scripts:

1. Save the script to a text file.

2. Download and install Awk or Perl.

3. Save price data to a text file – one price to a line.

4. Follow the instructions that came with Awk or Perl to execute the script (use the price file as an argument).

Awk Script

Here is the Awk script:

```
BEGIN   {
            control = 2000
            cash = control
            orig = control
        }

        {
          price = $1
          value = shares * price + cash
          shares = int(control / price)
          cash = value - shares * price
          if (cash < 0)
          {
             value += -1*cash
             orig += -1*cash
             cash = 0
          }
          print price"        "shares"         "cash"
"value" "orig
        }
```

If you want to use a constant value other than 2000, you need to edit the second line (control = 2000).

You can access this script online at
http://unix-simple.blogspot.com/2006/07/awk-program-for-trading-stocks.html

Perl Script

Here is the Perl script:

```perl
$cash = 2000;
$control = $cash;
$orig = $cash;

open(INFILE,$ARGV[0]) || die "Cannot open";

while (<INFILE>)
{
  $count++;
  chomp;
  $price = $_;
  $value = $shares * $price + $cash;
  $shares = int($control / $price);
  $cash = $value - $shares * $price;
  if ($cash < 0)
  {
     $value += -1*$cash;
     $orig += -1*$cash;
     $cash = 0;
  }
  print "$price    $shares $cash   $value
$orig","\n";
}
```

If you want to use a constant value other than 2000, you need to edit the first line ($cash = 2000;**).**

You can access this script online at:

http://unix-simple.blogspot.com/2006/07/perl-version-of-stock-trading-system_20.html

Example Price File

Here is an example of a price file:

```
10
20
5
10
```

When you run this file with either the Awk or Perl script, you should get the following output:

10	200	0	2000	2000
20	100	2000	4000	2000
5	400	500	2500	2000
10	200	2500	4500	2000

The columns are (from left to right): price, number of shares, cash pool, value, and amount invested.

Part VI – Reference

Feedback

I am very passionate about simplicity and my trading system. It has been a joy to write this book!

I really want to stay in touch with my readers. I welcome all comments, questions, and feedback!

You can email me at

StockTradingRiches [at] yahoo.com

You can also keep in touch through my blogs:

http://simple-trading-system.blogspot.com/

http://tao-simple.blogspot.com/

P.S. I would love to hear your opinion on whether interactive products (i.e. seminars, webinars, DVDs, etc) could help you learn my system better.

P.P.S. I am open to JV (Joint Venture) offers.

If you are interested in being an affiliate, please visit http://www.StockTradingRiches.com/affiliates.html for details.

Resources

http://simple-trading-system.blogspot.com/

http://www.StockTradingRiches.com/

http://tao-simple.blogspot.com/

http://unix-simple.blogspot.com/

http://www.barchart.com/

http://www.forbes.com/

http://moneycentral.msn.com/investor/home.asp

About the Author

Over the years, Praveen Puri has developed a passion for simplicity, minimalism, and Eastern philosophy.

He also has had a lot of financial and trading experience:

- *He has traded his own account for almost 20 years.*

- *As a consultant for a large insurance company, he helped design and implement custom software to track a $30 billion investment portfolio.*

- *As a consultant at the Chicago Board of Trade (CBOT), he helped support and develop their "Project A" electronic trading platform.*

- *He is currently a vice president at a major bank, where he supports and develops FX systems for corporate clients.*

Praveen lives in the Chicago area with his wife (Rasika), son (Anshul), and 2 cockatiels (Mickey and Donnie).

Part VII – 2009 Updates

How Did My System Perform During The Recession?

Before 2008, my account was averaging a double digit annual return. My returns for 2005, 2006, and 2007 were +13%, +14%, and +22%, respectively.

Then, in 2008, my account ended up down 40%, which was slightly worse than the S&P 500, which was down 38.5%. 2008 was one of the worst years since the Great Depression.

I did not panic, followed the Stock Trading Riches system, and simply rebalanced my positions in December 2008. I needed to add a lot of cash and did not have enough, so I actually had to follow the rule in the middle of page 24, and had to sell off some of my stocks to rebalance the others ("triage").

This year, as of November 17, 2009, my account is up 42% for the year!

Assuming the market does not tank in December, I will have achieved an average annual return of 6% over the five year period from 2005-2009. The S&P 500 average annual return is negative over this same period.

It's true that 6% is no longer double-digit, but we have to keep this in perspective: In the WORST 5-year period for stocks since the Great Depression, I still achieved a higher return than other asset classes (e.g. bonds, T-bills, money market funds)!

Now, past performance is no guarantee of future results, but my confidence and belief in the Stock Trading Riches trading system has only increased.

Get Three Free Trades From Scottrade

On page 23, I mentioned that I use Scottrade because they only charge $7 per trade.

I am still using Scottrade because I have found them to be very reliable, and their website is very easy to use.

Now, I can offer readers three free trades if they open a Scottrade account. Just use referral code ZNTJ5666.

Following A Proven Path To Make Money

I received a negative email from a Stock Trading Riches reader who complained that my system contained nothing new and exciting.

He missed the point of my system. It works because it pulls together old, "boring", but proven techniques. This illustrates why people reject simple and proven principles for building wealth, and turn instead to low percentage and high risk gambles.

When I was younger, the search for get-rich-quick excitement cost me a heck of a lot of money (both actual and from lost opportunity). That experience led me to developing trading systems based on proven principles.

For example, there is absolutely nothing new about re-balancing formulas. But they work - they have a sound basis and an edge. They trade volatility at the stock level, and capture compounding and growth at the portfolio level.

This is the type of investment system that people need for building wealth: A safe, non-leveraged system that buys low, sells high, and lets you compound and build your money over time.

The average investor does not need a complex system that offers the latest whiz-bang, cutting edge technical trading indicators. There is no need for mathematical "gymnastics".

Don't look for systems that are new-fangled and exciting. Instead, look for systems that you could recommend to your mother, and still sleep peacefully at night.

Trading systems are not meant to entertain and dazzle. They aren't designed to teach something "sexy" to brag about at cocktail parties. They are meant to make you money.

Could I Provide An Excel Spreadsheet For The "Stock Trading Riches" Formula?

Back on page 49, I provided Awk and Perl scripts to test my formula. Since I am used to working on Unix systems, I naturally used these scripts while testing and developing my system.

A reader at a hedge fund then wrote to me and asked if I had an Excel spreadsheet version. I realized that many financial and business people use Excel, so I took it as a challenge to create one.

The new Excel spreadsheet can be downloaded from either of these two links:

http://www.box.net/shared/u4g38s5ztx

http://snipurl.com/getspreadsheet

To Use The Spreadsheet:

1. Save a backup copy of the spreadsheet.

2. Open the spreadsheet with Microsoft Excel, Microsoft Office, or Open Office.

3. Enter the price sequence you want to test into the first column. The basic Stock Trading Riches system uses yearly prices, but you can also test daily, weekly, monthly, etc. prices.

4. Copy / paste to create more rows, if needed.

5. The other columns will show you the number of shares owned, cash balance, account total, and how much was invested.

6. The spreadsheet assumes that you start investing with $2,000.

7. You can get stock prices from sites such as BarChart.com.

8. If you have any questions, please email me at StockTradingRiches [at] yahoo.com.

Can You Use Mutual Funds With The "Stock Trading Riches" System?

Under "Complete System Rules" on page 23, I mentioned that I don't use mutual funds - only stocks or exchange traded funds (ETFs).

As a result, several readers have emailed me asking if they could use mutual funds with the Stock Trading Riches system.

The answer is that you can, but it's better to use stocks and/or ETFs because they have more volatility and certain tax advantages. See page 72 for more information.

Updated AMZN Stock Trading Example

Here is the updated Amazon.com (AMZN) trade example from page 20. It now includes the results from 2008 and 2009.

Remember that we pretended to initially buy 30 shares of AMZN at $64.56 in January, 2000. This was the WORST possible time – just before the dot-com crash.

We then turned over the management of this position to the Stock Trading Riches formula.

Here are the buys/sells that the formula would have recommended in January of each year:

2000	Buy 30 shares	@ $64.56
2001	Buy 85 shares	@ $17.31
2002	Buy 25 shares	@ $14.19
2003	Sell 49 shares	@ $21.85
2004	Sell 52 shares	@ $50.40
2005	Buy 7 shares	@ $43.22
2006	No Trade	@ $44.82
2007	Buy 7 shares	@ $37.67
2008	Sell 28 shares	@ $77.70
2009	Buy 5 shares	@ $58.82

Even though AMZN went down 9% from 2000 to 2009, the formula is up 80%. It mechanically "self-corrected" our bad timing.

Another Example of the "Stock Trading Riches" Formula

Let's pretend that we initially bought 142 shares of the India Fund (IFN) at $14.07 in January, 2005 and then turned over the management of this position to the Stock Trading Riches formula.

Here are the buys/sells that the formula would have recommended in January of each year:

2005	Buy 142 shares	@ $14.07
2006	Sell 72 shares	@ $28.27
2007	No Trade	@ $28.61
2008	Sell 19 shares	@ $39.05
2009	Buy 66 shares	@ $16.97

Even though IFN went _up 21%_ from 2005 to 2009, the formula is _up 82%_.

Would I Provide More Advice on Stock or Fund Selection?

Originally, on page 24, I provided only a little advice about selecting stocks.

Good stock picking will enhance your results, but the beauty of the "Stock Trading Riches" system is that it self-corrects your positions. The only requirement is to diversify among companies that will stay in business.

However, readers have indicated that they would like more information. I have also noticed that some of the most popular posts on my Simple Trading system blog (http://simple-trading-system.blogspot.com/) have been the ones where I analyze stocks.

Therefore, in the rest of this section, I have included articles on stock analysis, funds, and markets.

You can also read my blog to get stock picks. In the near future, I will launch a monthly newsletter to analyze stocks and the market. When I do, you will be able to sign up from my blog.

Again, remember that following the articles and stock picks are optional. You can choose to keep things simple and just feed well-established stocks to my system. The formula will self-correct the position over time, so you do not need to worry about correct timing.

Don't Let the Financial Crisis Scare You! The Hidden Dangers of Investing Too Conservatively

After witnessing 2008's financial crisis, many people are now tempted to avoid the stock market, and invest their money in CD's, money markets - maybe even their mattresses! This has its own risk and dangers.

The biggest risk is that you will not save enough to maintain your lifestyle in retirement. You may have to work full time - even if your health and other circumstances make that difficult.

If you invest safely in stocks, you can expect to earn at least 5% a year after inflation (the Stock Trading Riches system should average even more). Conservative non-stock investments, on the other hand, might earn 2% after inflation.

Thus, in order for your investments to generate your yearly salary without tapping into the principal, a stock portfolio would need to be 20 times your salary - while a non-stock portfolio would have to be 50 times your salary!

For example, a $50,000 salary is 5% of a $1,000,000 portfolio and 2% of a $2,500,000 portfolio.

Therefore, the reality is that, no matter how scary the short-term economy looks, you need to invest a substantial portion of your assets in stocks and/or stock funds. As long as you shun leverage, avoid speculative stocks with no earnings, and diversify, you can safely grow your money.

7 Stock Market Secrets For New Investors

Are you new to stock market investing? Fear not - investing is one of the best ways to build up your wealth and savings! It's also never too late to get started.

Here are 7 secrets for success:

1. *Don't be in a hurry or impatient* - this is especially true if you are getting started late. Even though there is an advantage to starting your investments while young, the truth is that anybody can begin seeing the effects of wealth building over 5 years or more. The secret is to remember that slow and steady wins the race. Let your wealth build up at its own pace. Trying to force things can result in loss though risky trades and excessive trading expenses.

2. *Diversify your holdings* - It is foolish to put all your money in one stock. If you do not have enough funds to put at least $2,000 in 5-10 stocks, then avoid individual stocks and stick with mutual funds or ETFs.

3. *Don't be an "all or nothing" trader* - After you decide on a certain allocation for a stock or fund, avoid putting the whole position on at once. Also avoid selling a whole position at one time. Work your way into and out of positions. You never know what a stock will do next. If you want to take profits or cut down on a loss, consider removing part of your position, but leave some shares in case the position goes up. The Stock Trading Riches system does this automatically.

4. *Avoid risky stocks* - you want to avoid penny stocks and stocks that are not making any money. If someone

tells you that a stock is going up, don't buy into it unless you understand what the company does and what it's advantage is. If you cannot determine this, then there is a good chance that the stock is going up on speculation.

5. *Select solid growth and value stocks* - Growth stocks are stocks that bring something new to the market and therefore have a legitimate reason to increase in value. Value stocks are stocks that are currently priced low to their income and/or assets. The best way to find these stocks consistently is to identify websites (e.g. Yahoo Finance) or magazines (e.g. Forbes) that have articles by respected analysts who explain the reasons behind their selections.

6. *Consider using a re-balancing system* - Good re-balancing systems, such as Stock Trading Riches, will use formulas to objectively pull money out of stocks when they are overvalued and put more money in when stocks are cheaper. Of course, no formula has perfect timing, but they are good enough to give you an edge over the long term.

7. *Avoid short term trading and technical-analysis* - Most people can not successfully predict markets over the short run, especially by looking at charts.

Divorce of a Trader - The Perils of Leverage

One day, when I was consulting at the Chicago Board of Trade, I overheard two traders talking about "Mike", who was an independent trader. His wife had finally gotten tired of their up and down finances, and she divorced him.

Just like any other trading system, Mike's system would sometimes produce losing trades. The problem was that Mike did not use a reasonable position size, and did not set money aside from wins. His money was always on the line. He and his wife literally moved from an apartment, to a big house, back to an apartment, back into a house and, after they lost their second house, she left him.

His story is important because, unfortunately, these types of tales are more common than the ones about someone getting rich overnight. People get interested in speculative trading (i.e. options, futures, day trading, stocks on margin, etc) because, in their heads, they calculate the possibilities of making a large return in a small amount of time.

What people fail to understand is that, if you trade a position that is large relative to your account size, you can just as easily make a large loss in a small amount of time. If, for example, you leverage a position so that your account doubles when the underlying market goes up 10%, then you are also setting up for your account to get wiped out if the market goes down 10%.

When your account becomes sensitive to changes of 10% or less, then you lose the ability to tolerate random fluctuations. When this occurs, having a well developed trading system with an edge is not enough - you are also dependent on short-term luck.

Ideally, a trader or investor will be disciplined, and never over-leverage his or her position. If you leverage your position even once, and succeed, it becomes hard not to try again. The problem then is that a trader may be able to successfully "push the envelope" once or twice, but it will eventually bite them.

With the Stock Trading Riches system, I do not use any leverage (e.g. borrowed funds or margin) because I don't want my system's edge wiped out by random fluctuations.

Why Stocks Are Better Than Mutual Funds

Many financial analysts tout mutual funds as being superior to direct investment in stocks. However, for accounts of $16,000 or more, investing in stocks can provide a much better risk-return profile.

Smaller accounts are better off with ETFs because they lack the capital to adequately diversify in stocks. An investor needs to hold a minimum of 8-10 stocks, and have a constant value of at least $2,000 per stock to keep expenses low with a discount broker.

The two biggest disadvantages of funds are:

1. *Lack of volatility.* Funds hold a large selection of stocks. Their individual movements tend to cancel each other out, thus dampening volatility. As a result, funds do not rise and fall as sharply as individual stocks. This applies to both mutual funds and ETFs.

In other words, when comparing a fund to an individual stock, the stock will have larger trading opportunities. A well-designed stock trading system (like my system) will trade each stock individually with a proven technique to buy low and sell high. (Safety is provided through portfolio diversification).

2. *Lack of tax control.* Investors who keep mutual funds in taxable accounts have no control over capital gains. The fund managers determine which securities to sell, when to sell them, and they choose the timing of capital gains distributions.

A stock or ETF trader, on the other hand, has several tools to manage taxes and boost his or her return. First, the trader can hold off on selling appreciated stock or ETF shares until it qualifies as a long-term capital gain (with a reduced tax rate).

Second, a trader can choose either a First In - First Out (FIFO) or Last In - First Out (LIFO) basis for matching buys and sells.

Third, a trader can "harvest capital losses" by completely selling a stock that is down in value (creating a capital loss to offset gains) and replacing it with a similar but different stock (i.e. substitute HP for IBM).

These techniques are detailed in the "Taxes" chapter, which starts on page 26.

Exchange Traded Fund (ETF) Investment Success - Stick to the Basics!

In the history of financial products, exchange traded funds (ETFs) were the fastest ones to reach popularity. After about 15 years, they now have $450 billion in assets.

Like a mutual fund, an ETF offers diversification in one package. Unlike a mutual fund, an ETF trades all day on a stock exchange - as if it were a share of stock.

The original batch of ETFs were like mutual funds, in that they represented a diversified portfolio of stocks. Unlike mutual funds, the ETFs do not actually buy and sell shares of stock. Instead, ETF shares are created by swapping new paper shares for baskets of stocks. Thus ETFs do not have to pay out capital gains like mutual funds and tend to be lower cost and tax efficient.

Therefore, traditional stock-based ETFs are a great trading and investment vehicle.

However, investors might want to think twice about the new-fangled exotic ETFs that are now hitting the market. These new ETFs tend to either represent leveraged stock indexes or physical commodities. These ETFs suffer from a narrow focus, high leverage, misleading labeling, and tax inefficiency:

1. *Narrow Focus* - As an example, The United States Oil Fund is supposed to track the West Texas Intermediate Crude Oil futures market. But it under performs the market due to slippage, since it is a very thin market.

2. *High Leverage* - The ETFs from ProShares trade 2 or 3 times the underlying index (or its reverse). However, these funds replicate 2 or 3 times the DAILY movement - not the movement over time. As a result, they may not work the way you expect. For example, The Ultra Oil and Gas ETF is a leveraged fund that moves in the direction of oil prices. The UltraShort Oil and Gas ETF is a leveraged fund that moves the opposite of oil prices. You would think that, in any given year, one fund would have a loss and the other fund would have a gain. But, because they only track the index on a day to day basis, both funds had double digit losses last year.

3. *Misleading Labeling* - The First Trust Global Wind Energy ETF sells itself as clean-energy. But the pool of wind-energy companies is so small, the fund has to own shares in BP and Royal Dutch Shell to maintain liquidity.

4. *Tax inefficiency* - Many metal ETFs, like the SPDR Gold Shares and iShares Silver Trust, are structured as grantor trusts and result in you paying taxes at ordinary income levels - rather than at capital gains rates.

Understanding the Difference Between International and Global Funds

If you invest in funds or ETFs, remember that the terms global and international are not interchangeable. Even though both types of funds invest in stocks from more than one country, there is a difference:

Global funds consist of stocks from many different countries -- including the investor's own country.

International funds also consist of stocks from different countries. But, by definition, they do not include companies based in the investor's home country.

Within these 2 broad categories, funds can be further classified according to market sector or industry. Thus, for example, there could be a global health fund, international durable goods fund, global steel fund, etc.

Global funds can be the right choice for investors who are just starting to build their portfolios, and do not have a lot of money to split up among many funds. By investing in a global fund, they can invest simultaneously in both the largest companies in their home country, as well as diversify in other countries.

On the other hand, an investor who already has a portfolio invested heavily in domestic stocks -- and wishes to diversify geographically -- will probably want to look at international funds. This is especially true for Americans, because U.S. multinational companies tend to have large market caps and have a heavy weighting in U.S. global funds.

It is important for fund investors to choose at least one of these funds, because some exposure to international securities is essential in today's globally connected economy. Individual parts of the world are vulnerable to slumps in their home economies, and capital is always shifting, seeking to move operations to low-cost countries, and tap world-wide pools of talent.

Combining Fundamental and Technical Analysis for Stock Trading

Most traders typically fall into one of two camps: fundamental or technical.

Fundamental analysis looks at economic / financial data (e.g. cash flow or price-earnings ratio) and news - at the levels of both the company and general economy.

For example, Forbes Magazine once recommended Canadian National Railroad because they have exclusive rail access to the new container terminal at the Port of Prince Rupert in British Columbia. This terminal should capture more freight traffic to Asia because it is 10 days from Shanghai vs. 12 days from the Port of Los Angeles.

The advantage of fundamental analysis is that it can help traders avoid trendless stocks in favor of those about to move significantly. The disadvantage is that fundamental analysis does not give precise buy and sell points, so it is hard to develop a testable, repeatable trading system. A lot of fundamental investors use buy and hold.

Technical analysis uses charts, indicators, and formulas based on stock price and/or trading volume. Pure technicians believe that studying fundamental information is not necessary because the market's reactions to the data will be reflected in the stock price.

The advantage of technical analysis is that it gives precise buy and sell signals that can be incorporated into a testable and repeatable system. The disadvantage is that market noise can cause traders to over-trade and get whipsawed (i.e. buy high and sell low for small losses) until the markets make a substantial move.

In my case, I use fundamental analysis (from sources such as Forbes) to add stocks to my portfolio, and then use the technical Stock Trading Riches system to make buy and sell decisions.

This way, I get the best of both worlds and have a double edge:

1. Fundamental analysis results in my portfolio getting invested in stocks that are stronger than the general market.

2. My formula self-corrects the initial buy points in each stock, so that I buy low and sell high based on the stock's actual performance.

Which Stocks Should You Be Investing In Now?

The bursting of the real estate bubble and sub-prime mortgages triggered a stock market meltdown and the "Great Recession" of 2008. Today, the recession is ending and stocks are off their lows. What stocks should you be investing in now?

Well, during the recession, investors not only fled stocks in general, but they also switched from small and weak companies into larger stocks with stable earnings. As a result, most of the recent gains in the stock market have been in these small and weak companies - since they were the most oversold.

Also, emerging markets have made a lot of gains, because their economies have started to recover before the U.S. Thus, at this time (fall 2009), it may be a good idea to avoid small company and emerging market stocks since they are up sharply and there is still uncertainty in the economy.

Some economists feel there is a danger of a second dip because unemployment is still high, and credit markets are still not fully open to small businesses and individuals. The most pessimistic economists feel that the United States is still in a deflationary market - where people will only buy if prices are slashed in "Cash for Clunkers" type deals. This would make it hard for companies to grow profits or hire back workers.

One safe bet might be for investors to look towards large stocks - especially industrial and health-care (despite the uncertainty around health care reform).

Health care is recession-proof, and big industrial stocks still haven't run up a lot. Thus they offer downside protection and, on the upside, are poised to soar if the economy further recovers.

An addition, there are other stocks to consider, depending on whether the economy is headed for high inflation, or possibly deflation…

How to Invest in an Era of High-Inflation and a Weak US Dollar

After years of monetary expansion, and now bailouts, there is the possibility that, once the recession is over, will see a devaluation of the U.S. dollar, possibly followed by inflation.

How should investors guard against this outcome?

U.S. stocks will eventually gain against inflation - but may lag by a decade. Also, if the U.S. dollar is devalued, then all U.S.-based assets will lose substantially.

Treasury bills hardly pay anything after inflation. Even Treasury Inflation-Protected Securities (TIPS) will under-perform unless held in tax-sheltered accounts.

Gold and silver are better hedges against war and crisis than inflation. In the last 34 years, the purchasing price of gold has only climbed about 2.7% per year - before insurance and assay costs.

A better alternative for hedging against both the risks of inflation and dollar devaluation might be to invest in the stocks of commodity producers with a lot of overseas sales.

At the start of inflationary periods, products such as copper, uranium, oil, and agriculture tend to perform best. Gold, on the other hand, tends to advance at the later, more speculative stages.

Therefore, if you think that inflation is about to kick in, you might want to start buying the stocks of companies involved in the international sales, mining and production of the above commodities.

Some possible examples include Archer Daniels Midland (agriculture), Southern Copper (copper), Cameco (uranium), Titanium Metals (titanium), and Viterra (agriculture).

Note that, except for Southern Copper (which is based in Peru), all the above companies are based in the U.S. and Canada. However, they have substantial foreign product sales and own undeveloped land. Both of these make excellent inflation hedges.

However, there is another scenario to also consider and maybe hedge for...

The "Great Recession," Deflation, and Stock Picking

The bursting of the real estate bubble and sub-prime mortgages triggered a stock market meltdown and the "Great Recession" of 2008. Today, the recession is ending and stocks are off their lows, but prices of goods and services have yet to recover.

There is a strong chance that, instead of inflationary growth, we are entering a deflationary period that may persist for a long time.

How will this affect successful stock picking?

There are structural changes behind the unwillingness and inability of consumers to spend more: highly paid manufacturing jobs have permanently disappeared, retirement accounts were devastated, and the easy credit and home equity loans fueling consumer spending have been tightened.

Retailers across the board - including sellers of luxury goods - have been forced to cut their prices. Consumers are aggressively hunting for deals, clipping coupons, and haggling.

In this type of market scenario, here are some things to look for in a potential stock investment:

1. *High-margin service providers vs. commodity sellers* - Manufacturers of PC's, for example, are experiencing falling prices and profits. Companies like IBM and HP, however, lead the way in offering high-margin consulting and integration services. They can under-price their computer systems relative to Dell because

they can use their hardware as "loss leaders" to acquire service clients.

2. *The health care industry* - Despite the uncertainty about health care reform, sickness is recession-proof. Pharmaceutical and medical supply companies have barriers to entry, with potential competitors held up by patents and needing FDA approval.

3. *Manufacturers of specialized components* - Any company that makes specialized equipment, i.e. deep-sea drilling bits, giant mining trucks, etc.

4. *Retailers with innovative logistics* - Walmart has an innovative supply and logistics chain. Amazon.com can thrive on lower prices because of it's famous negative operating cycle. For example, suppose that Best Buy and Amazon can both get iPods on net 45 day terms. If Best Buy turns its inventory over after 75 days, it must borrow funds for 30 days to pay Apple. In the case of Amazon, if it can turn its inventory over in 20 days, it can invest the money for 25 days before paying back Apple.

5 *High quality brands* - Even though luxury brands are experiencing some pricing pressures, the best brands have a "price floor" because they are perceived to be in a category by themselves. Examples include Apple and iPods, Gucci, Rolex, Mercedes-Benz, etc.

How Markets React to News and Reports

Markets that are freely traded, such as those for stocks, bonds, futures, and options, do not always react to fundamental news and reports the way a normal person might think.

For example, in August 2008, Burger King (BKC) reported its earnings. They greatly exceeded the earnings guidance that Burger King's executives had previously provided to analysts.

Based on these higher than expected earnings, one might expect that the stock went up. Instead, the stock went down sharply because, since their predictions were so far off, investors no longer felt that BKC management had any credibility.

As another example, Forbes columnist Ken Fisher has written about the "Presidential Stock Market Effect". Conventional wisdom might suggest that, when a Democrat is elected as president, the stock market should perform badly, because Republicans are more pro-business.

In actuality, the stock market has historically performed better during the inaugural years of Democrats, compared to Republicans. This is because of "reversion to the mean" - which is a key to contrarian trading.

The market expects the worst from a Democratic president when he takes power, but is then pleasantly surprised when they see that he maintains the status quo. In the same way, investors have high hopes that a Republican president will be pro-business. They expect the best, and get disappointed.

This is what makes trading on fundamental data very tricky. Not only do you need accurate and timely information, but you have to "out think" other market participants.

Like chess, you have to think many moves ahead, and try to piece together a puzzle based not only on what has just happened, but how other players will react, what actions they will take, etc.

The Problem With Trading From Charts - The Secret Flaw That Technical Analysts Never Talk About

A popular form of analysis is charting - where traders and investors examine price charts, looking for patterns that they believe can signal what will happen next in a given market or stock.

Analysts get especially excited about classical formations such as head-and-shoulders and sideways channels because, on historical charts, these patterns tend to stand out, well-formed, just before major market moves. They look as if they would have given a clear trading signal, enabling the trader to ride the trend to profits.

Unfortunately, there is a charting flaw that nobody really talks about. Because of this flaw, the patterns you see in hindsight would probably not have shown up during real time trading.

This flaw is a result of chart scaling. Charting software and chart books always scale the graph based on the highest and lowest prices. What this means is that, before a big move up or down, the chart scale will be over a smaller range. The chart will show more detail and more noise. After the move, however, when traders look back at the historical chart, the scale will now be set according to the new range. This means that *the price action just before the move will be now be drawn smoother with less noise*!

This is why, for example, breakouts from a sideways-channel look like an easy pattern for making money. If you look at charts of big moves, you see that price has moved in a tight, narrow channel and then broken out.

In reality, before the move happened, the chart scale would have been smaller, and the range of the sideways channel would have been the width of the whole chart.

A trader looking at the chart before the move would not see a tight sideways movement - instead, they would see a chaotic graph with lots of random up and down moves. If they tried to trade a breakout system, they would be whipsawed repeatedly and take enough small losses to cancel out much of the profit from the subsequent move.

This shows that chart patterns might not actually be caused by changes in supply/demand. Instead, they are just shapes formed by our minds that are dependent on scaling. Therefore, chart patterns may not give traders an edge.

The "zen" beauty of the Stock Trading Riches system is that it avoids these problems because it does not use charts or patterns. Instead, it focuses on the present moment - the rebalance point. The system does not care about the fluctuations that occur between one balance point and another.

Evaluate Trading Systems Critically - Be Wary of the Well-Placed Example

Before you use a particular trading system, you need to understand and critically evaluate it. This can save you both time, frustration, and your hard-earned dollars.

Here are three questions for evaluating a system:

1. Is the system "closed" ("black box") or "open" (white-box")? With a closed system, the owner of the system is only selling the trading advice that the system generates - not the system itself. This usually means that the you, as the buyer, will either get a program that spits out buys and sells, or else the system owner will email you buy and sell advice. You will not know anything about how the system works.

An open system, like Stock Trading Riches, fully discloses the rules, calculations, and logic that the system uses to make trading decisions. The trader can understand how the system should work under different market conditions, and he/she will be able to customize the system to match their risk/reward tolerance.

While a trader can still make money with a closed system, it will be a lot harder because you won't know when to expect loses, and you may not be able to control the risk. All trading systems will have periods where they have multiple losing trades in a row. If the trader does not have absolute faith and trust in his system, he or she may give up and look for a new system.

2. What is the system's edge? The edge is the advantage that the system has over chance - it is the reason that a trading system makes money over the long term. If a system does not have an edge then, over time, winning and losing trades would cancel each other out. If the edge cannot be explained in terms of economics, behavior, or mathematics, then there is a good chance that the edge does not exist. This is what makes trading with a black box system hard from a psychological standpoint.

3. Does the sample test data only consist of well-placed examples? This is one of the biggest issues with trading systems. The seller might only include sample trades that were placed under ideal conditions.

For example, one trading technique that people like are moving averages. This technique, however, does not work well in volatile markets. It works better in markets that trend either up or down. Someone selling a system based on moving averages should include sample trades under both trending and non-trending market conditions.

This is why I included the AMZN trade example in the book. This trade is actually initiated at the WORST possible price, and shows how the Stock Trading Riches system can self-correct stock positions over time.

If you are unsure about the sample data, then conduct an "out of sample" test. For example, if the system was tested using data from 1995-2005, then have the system performance tested with data from 2006-2008, or 1990-1994.

How To Select IPOs That Are Ready to Explode

A lot of traders and investors like to buy IPOs (initial public offerings) because they dream about buying the next Google or Microsoft before the stock price climbs.

Most companies, however, do not out-perform the market in the first year after they go public.

But there is a way to increase your chances of selecting IPO stocks that are hot and ready to climb.

This technique involves buying newly public companies that are market equals with companies that have already gone public - and whose shares have greatly increased since its IPO.

For example, on October 19, 2005, the Chicago Board of Trade (CBOT) went public. You would have bought this IPO because of the performance of it's rival, the Chicago Mercantile Exchange (CME).

Both CBOT and CME were two of the biggest futures exchanges in the world. They both had lots of trading volume, and were both raking in fees. The CME had gone public a year or so earlier, at $35-40. On 10/19/2005, it was trading in the 300s! There was no reason for CBOT stock to not behave similarly.

How did it work out? CBOT went public on 10/19/2005 with an IPO price of 54, but exploded! The stock opened at $80, hit a high of $85, and closed at $80. By the next year, CBOT was in the 200s. The CME eventually bought out CBOT, and shareholders ended up with CME stock around $490.

Another example of this technique was Visa (V). Visa went public on March 23, 2008. At that time, its rival, Mastercard, was trading at $223 - after going public in 08/06 around $40. Since Mastercard and Visa are roughly the same, there was good reason to suspect that Visa would do well too.

Visa ended up going public on 3/23/08 at $47, and reached $65 the next day. About a month later, on April 30, 2008, Visa reached $83.

In conclusion, then, a good technique is to buy IPOs of companies that have identical business models / market shares of companies that have gone public earlier, and outperformed the market. It's almost like being able to go back into time!

Stock Market Cap Analysis - Secrets For Building a Diversified Portfolio

Stocks can be separated into 4 groups, according to their market capitalization:

1. micro caps - below $300 million
2. small caps - between $300 million and $1 billion
3. mid caps - between $1 billion and $5 billion
4. large caps - over $5 billion

Market cap is calculated by multiplying the number of shares outstanding by the share price. For example, if stock ABC issued 6 million shares, and the price of each share is $6, then ABC has a market capitalization of $36 million.

In general, micro caps are new companies that are just hitting their stride. Small caps tend to have their infrastructure in place and are in growth mode. Mid caps are big regional or national companies. Large caps tend to be established multinational corporations.

Stocks within each market cap share important characteristics in the areas such as *growth rate, risk, dividends, visibility*, and *international exposure*.

It's important for investors to allocate their portfolios among all market caps to provide diversification, avoid cyclical returns, and take advantage of "regression to the mean" (e.g. one market cap segment outperforms another, but then they converge).

Let's look at market caps in more detail…

Stock Market Cap Analysis, Part I - Large Cap Stocks

Here are some of the characteristics of large caps:

1. Stability - Large cap stocks usually do not have the strong growth rates of smaller cap stocks, but they tend to have solid, stable earnings.

2. Visibility - Shares in large caps are widely held by the general public, large investors, pension funds, endowments, and mutual funds. They are usually covered by many analysts. Thus, these stocks are less risky and volatile than smaller cap stocks. The markets will usually uncover any problems with the business early, and warn investors ahead of time.

3. Dividends - Many large cap companies pay out their earnings as dividends. This fact makes them valuable holdings for investors seeking income (i.e. retirees).

4. International exposure - Large cap companies tend to do business globally. This provides geographic diversification for their operations and earnings. They are able to capitalize by moving operations to low-cost countries, and tapping world-wide pools of talent. They are not as dependent on slumps in their home economies.

Stock Market Cap Analysis, Part II - Medium Cap Stocks

Medium cap companies combine some of the traits of small caps with those of large caps:

1. *Stability* - Like large caps, many midcap stocks are not fast-growing, but they have earnings stability.

2. *Less well-known* - Medium cap stocks aren't household names like large caps tend to be. Thus, to a lesser degree, they share the small cap trait of not being extensively followed and analyzed. This means that they might provide more opportunity for buying under-priced shares. On the other hand, investors could find them more volatile. Also, since they are not as widely held, the market may not give signals when there are problems. Thus, investors may not get warnings ahead of time.

3. *Dividends* - Midcaps may not pay out as much in dividends as large-caps do. They should thus make up a smaller portion of portfolios for investors seeking income (i.e. retirees).

4. *Less international diversification* - Medium cap companies may lack the global diversification of large cap companies. They may be more affected by regional and national slumps. On the other hand, they may capture domestic market share from large cap leaders who focus too much attention on expanding abroad.

Stock Market Cap Analysis, Part III - Small Cap Stocks

Here are some of the features of small caps:

1. *High growth rates* - Small cap companies are usually in growth mode. Either they are selling a new product or service, or else they are well-established in a certain region and are looking to expand. This means that the stock price may appreciate a lot in the near future, as earnings and sales increase.

2. *Less well-known and analyzed* - Small caps are usually not extensively followed and analyzed by Wall Street. Most of their outstanding shares are not owned by mutual funds, pension plans, and endowments. This means that the stocks have more chances to be inefficiently priced, thus giving small investors more opportunities for buying under-priced shares.

3. *More risky* - Small cap stocks are riskier than medium and large cap stocks because they may not have the stable cash flow, deep management talent, clout, and lines of credit to weather strategic mistakes and/or down markets. Since the stocks aren't heavily followed and analyzed by Wall Street firms, investors may not learn about bad news before the share price fully reflects the information.

4. *Less insulated from stock market trends* - Not only do small companies themselves lack the resources to resist bear markets, but investor behavior itself exaggerates the effects of market conditions. Investors are quick to jump out of small caps when the market turns down, and they are quick to jump aboard during bull market runs.

Stock Market Cap Analysis, Part IV - Micro Cap Stocks

Micro cap stocks take the advantages and disadvantages of small cap stocks to an extreme:

1. *High potential growth rates* - Like small caps, micro caps are either selling a new product or service, or else looking to expand geographically. Unlike small caps, most micros haven't started to enjoy fast growth rates. They are still plodding along before they hit critical mass and take off. This means that investors have a chance to jump on-board early, and catch the full move.

2. *Less information and analysis* - While small caps may have some Wall Street analysis, micro cap stocks suffer from a dearth of information. They are almost never owned by institutional investors. On the plus side, this means that mis-priced bargains are relatively plentiful.

3. *Very risky* - Micro caps are the riskiest capitalization group because they are the most likely companies to lack stable cash flow, management talent, and infrastructure. They tend to be the most vulnerable to economic down turns and failed corporate strategy. Public investors may never have all the information necessary to sell off bad companies before the share prices tank.

4. *Illiquid trading* - Micro capitalization stocks may trade with thin volume. This increases trading expenses through wider bid-ask spreads. Since many micro caps do not trade on an exchange, retails brokers may charge extra commissions and/or fees. In the event of negative news, exiting a large position may be difficult and costly.

6 Unconventional Metrics For Stock Picking

You may want to use these 6 metrics, in addition to the conventional ones like book value and earnings, when evaluating stocks:

1. *Expansion* - Here we look at two things: the number of new employees added and the amount spent on fixed capital expenditures. For each one, compare the value from the latest quarter with that of the same quarter one year ago. Ideally, these numbers will increase.

2. *Productivity* - Divide sales by the number of employees, and see if it has increased between the latest quarter and the same quarter one year ago.

3. *Dividends* - Look at the dividend as a percentage of free cash flow (cash from operations less capital expenditures). If the dividend is more than 100% of FCF, then it is a sign of trouble.

4. *Pension Expectations* - For companies with pension plans, look at the return they use for calculating whether the plans are well-funded. If they assume an aggressive rate of return (i.e. 8.5%), then it is a red flag.

5. *Pension Surplus or Shortfall* - Be wary of companies that have large shortfalls in the funding of their pension plans.

6. *Pension Allocations* - It is a red flag if a high percentage of their pension plans are allocated to risky investments.

www.ingramcontent.com/pod-product-compliance
Lightning Source LLC
Chambersburg PA
CBHW081140170526

45165CB00008B/2737